WHICH IS DIFFERENT?

Please visit our website, www.garethstevens.com. For a free color catalog of all our high-quality books, call toll free 1-800-542-2595 or fax 1-877-542-2596.

Publisher Cataloging Data

Jeffries, Joyce
        Which is different? – 1st ed. / by Joyce Jeffries.
p.   cm. – (Dinosaur school)
Summary: Colorful dinosaurs introduce sorting.
ISBN 978-1-4339-8103-6 (hard bound) – ISBN 978-1-4339-8104-3 (pbk.)
ISBN 978-1-4339-8105-0 (6-pack)
        1. Set theory—Juvenile literature   [1. Set theory]   I. Title
                2013
      511.3/22—dc23

First Edition

Published in 2013 by
Gareth Stevens Publishing
111 East 14th Street, Suite 349
New York, NY 10003

Designer: Mickey Harmon
Editor: Katie Kawa

All illustrations by Planman Technologies

Printed in the United States of America

CPSIA compliance information: Batch #CW13GS: For further information contact Gareth Stevens, New York, New York at 1-800-542-2595.

WHICH IS DIFFERENT?

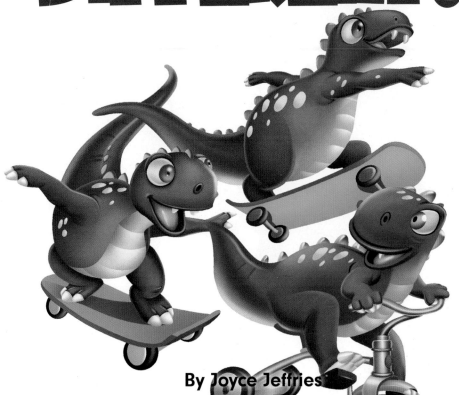

By Joyce Jeffries

Gareth Stevens
Publishing

Which is different?

The orange is different.

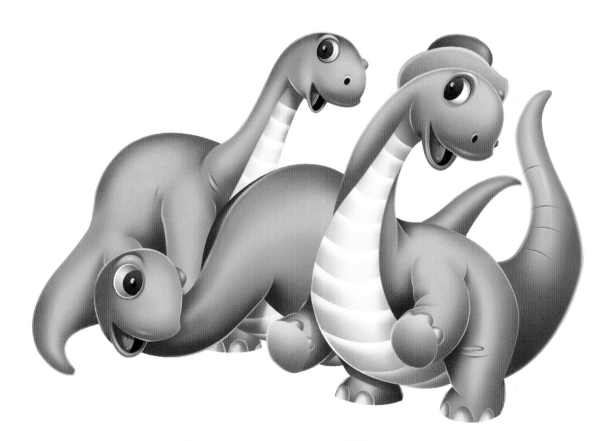

Which is different?

The hat is different.

Which is different?

The dog is different.

Which is different?

The book is different.

Which is different?

The shoes are different.

Which is different?

The ice cream is different.

Which is different?

The tricycle is different.

Which is different?

The fish is different.

Which is different?

The dress is different.

Which is different?

The kite is different.

Which is different?

24